STEP INTO THE WORLD OF
ANCIENT
GREECE

938
16790N

SOCIETY

CONTENTS

5   People

9   Daily Life

13   Games and Sports

17   Art and Craft

21   Theatre

CONTENTS

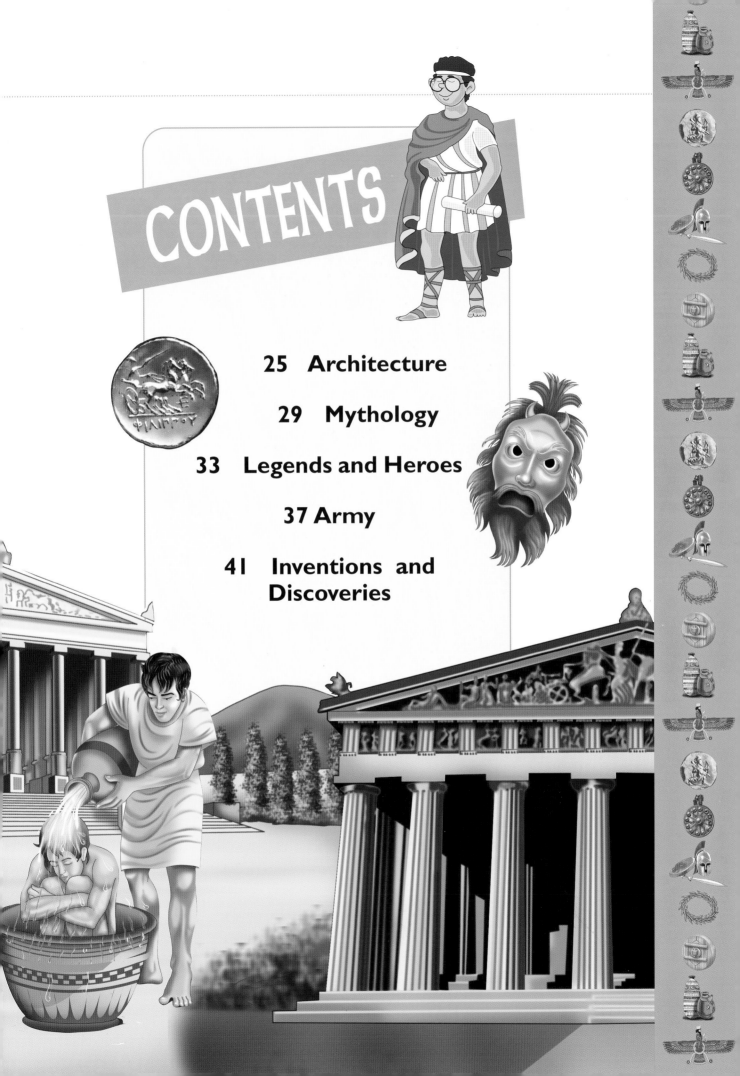

25   Architecture

29   Mythology

33   Legends and Heroes

37 Army

41   Inventions and Discoveries

PEOPLE

About 2,500 years ago, there lived a people who called themselves Hellenes, and their land, Hellas. They were the ancient Greeks. While some of them became famous as great thinkers others built beautiful buildings. They also developed a form of government which is used even today.

City or State?

The ancient Greeks lived in city-states. Each city-state was made up of a city or town, and the surrounding villages, and had its own rules and laws. Athens and Sparta were the most important city-states. They were often at war with each other since each wanted to be more powerful.

Votes and Verdicts

The Greeks could even vote against their leaders. A leader was sent into exile if 6,000 citizens wrote his name on the "ostrakon" (broken pottery pieces).

The judges used clay discs to announce their decisions. There were special discs for declaring "guilty" and "not-guilty".

What was a *polis*?

The ancient Greeks lived in city-states. Each city-state was an independent political unit and was called a *polis*.

Were serfs considered citizens?

Serfs, or farmers, were non-citizens. So were women and slaves. This meant that they did not have the right to vote.

Did the Greek city-states have different types of governments?

In ancient Greece, Corinth was first a tyranny (ruled by one dictator) and later an oligarchy (ruled by a group of people). Athens was a democracy, while Sparta was a monarchy.

Was Athens actually the first democracy?

The idea of democracy is believed to have begun in Athens because Athenian men could cast their votes and choose their leaders. However, only those men who were born in Athens and also owned property were allowed to vote. Athens also had a system called "ostracism", by which an unpopular person could be cast out from the city if enough votes against him were collected from the people.

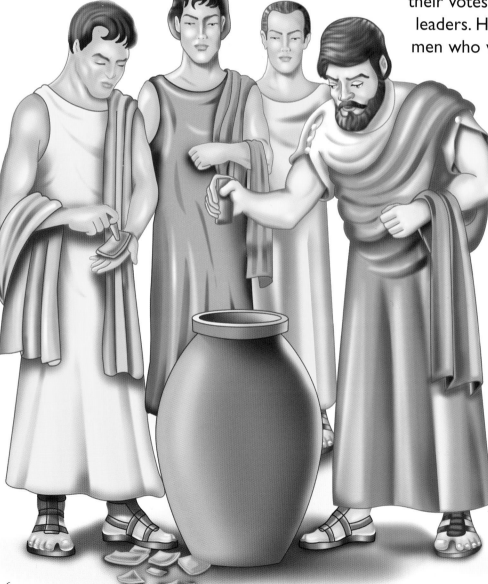

Early Athenians casting their vote

Did men and women have equal rights in Greek society?

In ancient Greece boys were given a formal education but girls were mainly taught at home. The main occupations of Greek women were weaving, spinning and managing the household. They were not allowed to vote.

A Greek woman making bread for her family

A captured slave

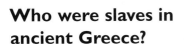

Who were the different types of Greek people?

Ancient Greece was made up of several city-states that had their own unique characteristics. Some of the various Grecian peoples were Athenians (from Athens), Spartans (from Sparta), Thebans (from Thebes) and Corinthians (from Corinth).

Who were slaves in ancient Greece?

Slaves in ancient Greece were usually either captured enemy soldiers or the children of slaves. Sometimes, slaves were kidnapped boys and men as well!

FACT BOX

■ The ancient Greeks called the non-Greek people "barbarians". The Greeks considered themselves the most civilised people in the world.

■ Athens was the largest city-state in ancient Greece. By 500-450 B.C., it had a population of close to 100,000.

■ Slaves in ancient Greece were often paid for their work. If they saved enough coins, they could even "buy" their freedom from their masters.

A slave could buy his freedom with coins

7

Who were regarded as citizens in ancient Greece?

Greek citizens were men who owned land and took part in the government. They were divided into various classes according to their family history and wealth.

Was music important to the ancient Greeks?

Folk songs and hymns were sung at ancient Greek festivals and religious events. Various musical instruments accompanied poetry recitals and dancing. Music was also an important subject in schools.

 Who framed the first laws in Greece?

Draco wrote down the first official set of laws in Greece. These laws were so severe that the word "draconic" is now used to describe something that is unduly harsh.

 Where does the word "politics" come from?

The word "politics" comes from the Greek word "politikos", meaning "of the city".

Did masters name their slaves in ancient Greece?

Slaves in ancient Greece were known by the names that their masters gave them. A slave was not allowed to have another name.

Ancient Greeks were very fond of music and dance

DAILY LIFE

The ancient Greek family was headed by the father. He took all important decisions. The mother raised the children and supervised the slaves.

Time to Eat

The Greeks ate bread, cakes and porridge. Cooking was done over charcoal fire, usually in clay or bronze utensils. The food was cooked in olive oil and sweetened with honey.

Going to School

Athenian boys went to school to learn arithmetic, reading and writing. Most girls learnt reading, weaving and cooking at home. Music schools trained students in playing the flute and the lyre.

In Sparta it was considered more important to learn how to fight wars. Even girls were trained in physical exercises.

Play and Party!

Children played with dolls and other toys made of pottery. While the mothers mostly stayed at home, the fathers spent a lot of time outdoors, talking with other men at the *agora* or at parties called "symposions".

Mother and daughter at home

A young pupil with his teacher

DAILY LIFE

Did Greek children have toys to play with?

A child playing with his pull-along toy

Ancient Greek children played with toys such as rattles, terracotta dolls, yo-yos and pull-along animals on wheels.

What did Greek children study at school?

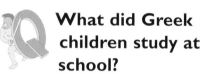

In most Greek schools, children first studied the works of the epic poet Homer and learnt to play the lyre. Later, their subjects included art, reading, writing, maths, drama, public speaking and government. Finally, they were trained at a military school. While most girls learnt at home only, in Sparta they went to schools to be trained in sports and military skills.

Why did Spartan boys leave home at the age of seven?

At the age of seven, Spartan boys were sent to military school. There they received extremely strict and harsh training. Now we use the word "spartan" to describe discipline or austerity.

What kinds of pets did ancient Greek families keep?

Greek families kept pets such as birds, dogs, goats, horses, tortoises and mice.

What did Greek people do at the *agora*?

The *agora* was an open area that contained important civic buildings and markets. People met, shopped and relaxed at the *agora*, which was laid out among trees, fountains and statues.

Shopping and chatting at the agora

How did Greek women style their hair?

Greek women usually had long hair, which they wore in plaits on top of the head, or tied into ponytails. Headbands were often used as hair ornament.

A fashionable Greek hairstyle

What was a *chiton*?

The Greeks wore a loose tunic called *chiton*, which was gathered at the waist with a belt. The *himation*, a woollen cloak, was draped over it.

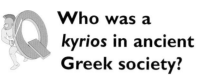

DAILY LIFE

Grapes and olives

Who was a *kyrios* in ancient Greek society?

The *kyrios*, or official guardian, of a woman was her father before she was married and her husband after marriage.

What musical instruments did ancient Greeks play?

Two popular Grecian musical instruments were the flute and the lyre. One type of lyre had the base made from a hollow tortoise shell, with an animal skin stretched over it.

How did a slave help his master take a bath?

During a shower, the slave poured water over his master, who used to be seated in a large pottery bowl.

Which two fruits are closely linked to the Greek civilization?

Olives and grapes were very important to the ancient Greeks. Olive oil was a vital part of their diet. Wine made from grapes was served at meals as well as on festive occasions.

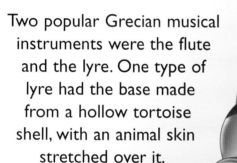

Greek man enjoying a cool shower

What did the ancient Greeks write on?

The ancient Greeks carved inscriptions on stone and pottery. They also used the papyrus, a kind of paper made from reeds. It was brought from Egypt. The Greeks also used parchment prepared from the skin of sheep and goats.

GAMES AND SPORTS

It is believed that the Greeks first organised sports events to mark important funeral ceremonies. Later, these were held during religious occasions as well.

The four major sports festivals were the Isthmian, Nemean, Pythian and Olympic games.

A crown of olive leaves

The Olympics

The Olympics were held at Olympia in honour of the god Zeus. The Greeks were known to measure time in terms of Olympiads - four-year periods between two games! Even wars used to be halted for the Olympics.

No Women, Please!

Married women were not allowed at the Olympics. This was probably because the athletes used to be naked !

Hip Hip Hooray!

The prizes at the Olympic, Isthmian, Nemean and Pythian games were, respectively, a crown of olive leaves, a crown of pine branches, a parsley crown and apples.

Apples for the winner

GAMES AND SPORTS

Which games were held in honour of the goddess Athena?

The annual Panathenaic Games in Athens were held in honour of Athena, the city goddess. The games had exciting events such as high-speed chariot races, in which a foot soldier would jump out of the vehicle towards the end of the race and sprint to the finish line.

Which was the shortest race at the ancient Olympics?

A sprint called the stade was the shortest race at the ancient Olympics. It was just about 192 metres (0.1 mile) long.

Did the ancient Olympics feature a race with a flaming torch?

The ancient Olympics had a relay race in which a team of riders on horseback carried a flaming torch.

What is the difference between the ancient and modern pentathlons?

The ancient pentathlon (from the Greek word for five - *pente*) comprised of wrestling, jumping, running, discus throwing and javelin throwing. The modern pentathlon features horse racing, fencing, pistol shooting, swimming and cross-country running.

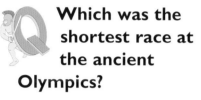

Greek athletes at the pentathlon

relay race with a
flaming torch

Where did people stay during the five-day festival at Olympia?

While important guests and athletes stayed in special rooms, the other visitors either pitched tents or slept in the open.

How did ancient Greek athletes improve their performance at long jump?

When launching into a long jump, ancient Greek athletes carried heavy lead or stone weights to cover a greater distance.

Which was the longest race at the ancient Olympic Games?

A foot race called *dolichos* was the longest race at the ancient Olympics. It was about 5 kilometres (3.1 miles) long.

15

GAMES AND SPORTS

 **What oath did the participants take before the Olympics commenced?**

The participants had to take an oath before a statue of Zeus, stating that they had trained for 10 months before the Olympic Games.

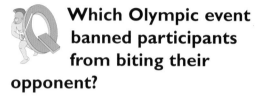 **Which Olympic event banned participants from biting their opponent?**

Participants at the pankration wrestling event were not allowed to bite or break the fingers of the opponent. They were also forbidden to hit the opponent in the eye. Otherwise, there were hardly any rules for this violent event.

A winner being treated to a banquet

 **In which events did women participate during the Heraia?**

Running races were the only events at the Heraia, and only unmarried women could take part in these.

A Greek woman runner

 What did Greek boxers wear on their hands?

Greek boxers wrapped strips of leather around their fists. They did not have the padded gloves of present-day boxers.

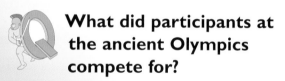 **What did participants at the ancient Olympics compete for?**

The participants competed for wreaths made of leaves from a sacred olive tree, located near the Temple of Zeus in Olympia. They were also treated to banquets and free meals!

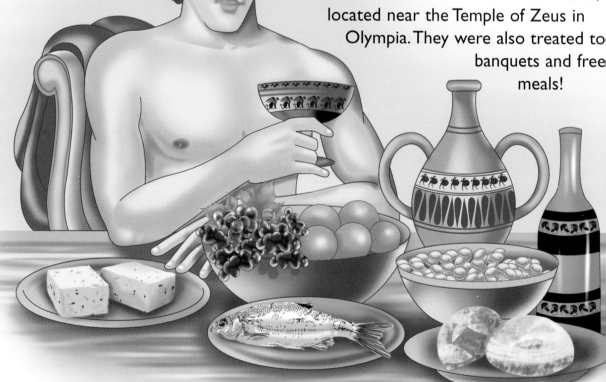

16

ARTS AND CRAFTS

Craftsmen in ancient Greece made many beautiful objects - from life-sized statues to bowls, cups, vases and jars. The objects were often painted with animals, people and scenes from daily life.

Red-figure pottery

Magic Paint

Corinth and Athens were famous for their red-and-black pots, which were decorated without any paint! The craftsmen used a water-clay mixture instead. These "painted" pots were also shipped abroad.

A Tale of Tales

The ancient Greeks used to listen to poets playing the lyre and singing tales of heroes, gods and goddesses. Besides stories and plays, Greek writers also wrote books on philosophy and history.

Let's Dance!

The Greek people had about 200 types of dances, for both happy and sad times.

The great poet Homer

ARTS AND CRAFTS

Who did the Muses help?

In Greek mythology, the Muses were nine goddesses who provided inspiration for the arts, literature and sciences. They had individual names and attributes - for instance, Euterpe, the Muse of lyric poetry, was portrayed with a double flute, while Melpomene, the Muse of tragedy, carried a tragic mask.

Melpomene, the Muse of tragedy

How did ancient Greek artists make their colours?

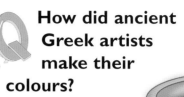

Greek artists created their colours from various materials. They made yellow, brown and red from clay and rocks; green from copper; white from chalk; purple from rare seashells; and blue from glass.

Why were ancient Greek pottery vessels of so many different shapes?

Greek potters made vessels of different shapes and sizes because they all had different uses. An *amphora* was used mainly for storing things; the three-handled *hydria* was for holding water; and *kylix* and *kantharos* were drinking cups.

What is the difference between red-figure and black-figure pottery?

The ancient Greeks were famous for their red-figure and black-figure pottery. The first has red figures on a black background, and the inner details were painted. In the other form, black patterns were outlined on a red-orange background, with the details carved on to the surface.

What is the Homeric Question?

The Homeric Question concerns the actual existence of Homer, the ancient Greek poet. He is widely held to be the author of two epics - the *Iliad* and the *Odyssey*. However, some people think that it was a group of people who wrote under that name.

ours used y Greek artists

How did Greek potters make such huge urns and vessels?

Large pottery vessels, such as pithoi, were probably first made in sections and then joined together before being fired.

Decorating pottery

FACT BOX

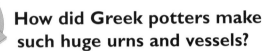

Greek Alphabets

■ The earliest Greek alphabet was taken from the Phoenician script, which was read and written from right to left. Later, the Greeks added new letters and changed the script to make it follow a left-to-right direction. The word "alphabet" itself comes from *alpha* and *beta* - the first two letters of the Greek alphabet.

■ Praxiteles, regarded as one of the greatest Greek sculptors, made the famous statue of the god Hermes in Olympia.

■ The ancient Greek sculptors and painters were the first to portray the human body in a life-like way.

ARTS AND CRAFTS

 Was the famous sculpture *Doryphorus* ("Spear Bearer") made of marble?

The original Doryphorus was made of bronze. The sculpture was lost, however, and all that we have now is a Roman copy of the statue in marble.

 Did the ancient Greeks make paintings to hang on walls?

The ancient Greeks did not hang paintings on walls. Instead, they painted figures and scenes on the walls.

How did ancient Greeks make mosaics?

The ancient Greeks were the first to make mosaic artworks. They stuck pieces of stone and glass - called tesserae - on to walls and floors.

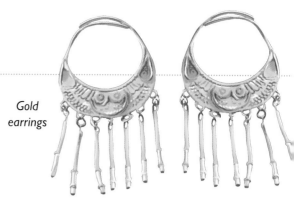

Gold earrings

 Was gold jewellery made in ancient Greece?

The ancient Greeks made beautiful earrings and pendants of gold. Some of the jewellery has been found in graves in Greece.

 What kind of jars was given as prizes at sports events?

Painted jars filled with olive oil were often given as prizes at athletic events.

Who made the statue of Zeus at Olympia?

Phidias made the huge statue of Zeus at Olympia. The master sculptor also made many sculptures at the Parthenon.

A worker creating a mosaic

THEATRE

In ancient Greece, plays were performed during the festival of Dionysus, the god of wine. Going to the theatre was a special occasion. Plays were staged all day long, at the end of which the writer of the best play was awarded.

It is said that women in ancient Greece were allowed to watch only tragedies!

A happy mask

At the Theatre

Greek theatres were large, semi-circular auditoriums built on the hillside. The audience sat on tiered seats around the stage. Even the people on the higher seats could hear the actors clearly.

Getting Musical

The chorus (group of singers) stood in an area in front of the stage. The musicians played the lyre, the syrinx (pan pipes) and the aulos (double flute).

Syrinx, a Greek wind instrument

Actors in Action

Initially, Greek plays had only one actor. He wore different masks for different roles. Since the plays were mostly religious, an actor played the role of various gods. A crane was used to lift him when he had to be shown as flying.

THEATRE

 Did Greek actors wear masks to disguise themselves?

Greek actors wore masks not to disguise themselves but to portray the characters they were playing. A single actor could act out different characters in the same play just by putting on different masks and clothes.

A mask worn by Greek actors

 Why were Greek actors called *hypokrites*?

In the first Greek plays, actors were brought in to answer the chorus. Hence they were called *hypokrites*, which means "answerer". The word "hypocrite" is now used for a person who is a fraud or puts on an act!

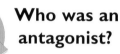 **What was the stage in ancient Greek theatres made of?**

While the earliest Greek theatres had a wooden stage, the later ones were made of stone.

Who was an antagonist?

Ancient Greek theatre started with one central actor called the protagonist. The dramatis Aeschylus is said to have introduce a second actor, called the antagonist, who interacted with the protagonist.

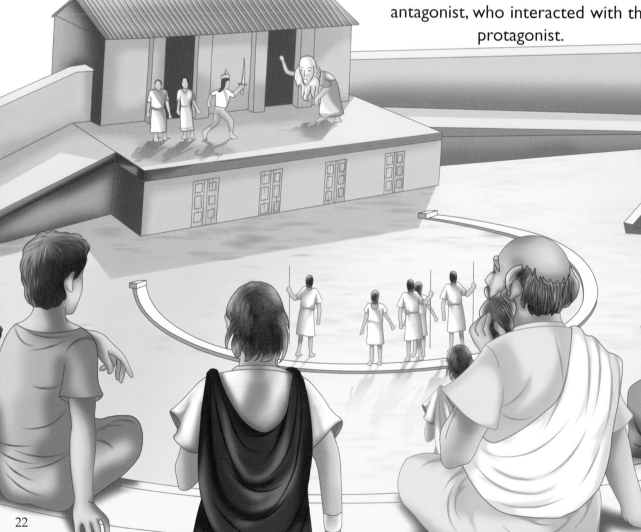

Who was Thespis?

The Greek poet Thespis is regarded as the creator of tragedy as well as the actor's part in drama. Thespis is also recorded as the first to win a drama competition, which was held in honour of the god Dionysus in 534 B.C. The word "thespian", which we now use for both actors and the dramatic arts, is derived from Thespis.

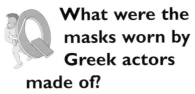

What were the masks worn by Greek actors made of?

Greek actors wore masks made of cork, carved wood, leather or strips of linen covered with plaster. Actors could portray different emotions by changing their masks, which were painted with various expressions.

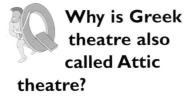

Why is Greek theatre also called Attic theatre?

Greek theatre is also referred to as Attic theatre because Athens, the place where Greek drama originated, was situated in a region called Attica.

Watching a play at the amphitheatre

FACT BOX

■ The Theatre of Dionysus in Athens had seats for about 17,000 spectators. Other important amphitheatres were the Attic Theatre and the theatre at Delphi.

■ Women were not allowed to act in Greek plays. Male actors enacted the women's parts as well! However, it is believed that women could watch the performances.

■ Aeschylus, Sophocles and Euripides were among the most distinguished dramatists who wrote tragedies. The playwright Aristophanes wrote comedies.

Greek playwright Sophocles

THEATRE

Who occupied the first few rows of seats in the theatre?

The first row in a Greek theatre was mostly reserved for priests. Officials and other important people sat in the rows behind the priests. The common citizens sat behind the officials.

A Greek actor's shoes

What kind of shoes did Greek actors wear?

The actors in ancient Greek plays wore thick-soled shoes called kothornoi, which reached up to the calf, and sometimes even the knee, of the wearer.

Where did the theatre actors change costumes?

The theatre actors changed their costumes in a room behind the stage. It was called the skene ("tent"). Actors could enter or leave the stage through a set of doors in the skene.

How did Greek actors dress for their performances?

Greek actors wore padded clothes for various reasons - to appear bigger to the audience, to look impressiveor even to appear silly. Actors in tragic plays dressed in long, flowing and richly designed robes. The colours of the costumes depended on what was being portrayed — bright colours showed happiness, black was for grief and hunters draped their left arm with a purple cloth.

Who was the first person to get the skene painted?

It is believed that Sophocles was the first person to get the skene painted, in order to use it as background scenery. In fact, the word "scene" comes from skene.

Greek actors wearing masks

ARCHITECTURE

The ancient Greek people lived in houses made of mud bricks. There was a courtyard in the centre and rooms were built around it. In some houses the floors and walls were decorated in colourful patterns called mosaics. These were made using multicoloured pebbles.

Sacred Secrets

The Greeks used the finest of materials and hired the best of craftsmen to erect magnificent temples. Marble statues were installed and the walls were decorated with paintings.

The temples had tall columns supporting the roof. While some columns were quite plain, others had elaborate designs carved on them. Large stone discs with pegs were fitted together to create each column!

Discs with pegs

The Parthenon

The Parthenon stands tall amongst Greek temples. This 5th-century-B.C. temple was built in honour of Athena, the goddess of war, after the Athenians won a war against Persia.

ARCHITECTURE

Which temple on the Acropolis is considered to be the finest?

The Parthenon is considered to be the finest temple on the Acropolis. It was built in honour of Athena Parthenos, the patron goddess of Athens, during the mid-5th century B.C. The Parthenon was made of white marble and had 46 columns.

Which temple on the Acropolis was dedicated to the Greek goddess of victory?

The Temple of Athena Nike was built around 425 B.C. in honour of the Greek goddess of victory. It had a marble parapet carved with images of Greek victories (*Nikae*).

The huge ivory and statue of Zeu

What were Caryatids?

Caryatids were decorative column-like supports built in the shape of female figures.

What were the "kourai" and "korai" statues?

In the Greek language, "kouros" (plural "kourai") and "kore" (plural "korai") refer to a youth and a young girl, respectively. Some ancient Greek statues were images of kourai and korai. Usually carved in marble, these were used mainly as headstones and memorials.

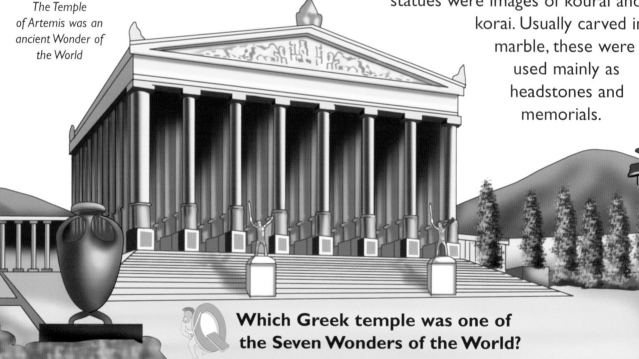

The Temple of Artemis was an ancient Wonder of the World

Which Greek temple was one of the Seven Wonders of the World?

The Temple of Artemis at Ephesus was one of the Seven Wonders of the World. The 106-columned temple was destroyed by invaders in A.D. 262.

Which Greek temple housed a statue that was one of the Seven Wonders of the World?

The Temple of Zeus at Olympia housed the Statue of Zeus, which was one of the Seven Wonders of the World. The ivory-and-gold statue, made by Phidias of Athens, is believed to have been almost 12 metres (40 feet) high. The temple no longer exists.

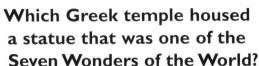

How was the Parthenon damaged in the 17th century?

The Parthenon was used as a gunpowder store by the Ottoman Turks who had occupied Greece. During a fight an explosion occured that badly damaged the roof and walls.

The magnificent Parthenon temple

Why were the columns of the Parthenon narrower at the top than at the base?

The columns of the Parthenon were built narrower at the top so that they would look straight when viewed from a distance.

FACT BOX

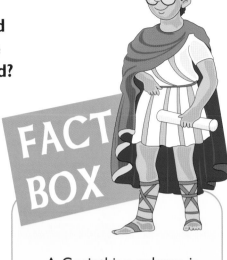

■ A Corinthian column is a type of pillar first used in Greek architecture. The top of the column was

Corinthian column

decorated with carvings of acanthus leaves.

■ The Acropolis was known as the "sacred rock" of ancient Athens. It was a hill in the middle of the city with a cluster of temples built on it.

■ The Colossus of Rhodes was destroyed in an earthquake about 225/226 B.C. This bronze statue, dedicated to the sun god Helios, stood about 36.5 metres (120 feet) high and was one of the Seven Ancient Wonders.

ARCHITECTURE

What were the roofs of ancient Greek houses made of?

Clay tiles were used to make the roofs of houses in ancient Greece.

Roof tiles made of clay

What were the covered areas in Greek markets called?

Greek markets (*agoras*) had covered areas called stoas along the edges. People could stroll in the shade or sit and talk to friends in the stoas.

How did the Greeks build the Parthenon?

The Greeks used the latest technology to build the Parthenon. Large blocks of marble and stone were first hauled to the site of the temple. Workers then used ropes and pulleys to lift up the slabs.

Pulleys being used to construct the Parthenon

Why did the Greeks have three legged stools and tables at their homes?

Greek homes had a bumpy, uneven floor. Tripods and other three-legged stools were used because they stood stable on such floor.

Which Greek columns were the simplest in design?

The Doric columns had the simplest design in ancient Greek architecture. The capital (topmost part) had no carvings.

MYTHOLOGY

People in ancient Greece believed in many gods. There were gods and goddesses for everything.

All in the Family

The Greeks thought that all the gods and goddesses came from one family. Zeus, the god of thunder, was the head of the family. He was married to the goddess Hera. Among their many children were Ares, the god of war and Athena, the goddess of war and wisdom.

Zeus with his thunderbolt

Pleasing Gods

Each god and goddess was supposed to be exceptionally good at one craft. While Artemis was an expert hunter, Dionysus was the god of wine and theatre. In order to please the gods, the Greeks built temples and sacrificed animals.

Divine Dialogue

The Greeks believed that gods and goddesses "spoke" to them. People visited oracles (holy places where a deity reveals knowledge through a priest or priestess) to consult the gods before taking any important decision.

MYTHOLOGY

 What escaped from Pandora's Box?

According to Greek myth, Zeus created the first woman, named Pandora. She had a box with her which she was asked not to open. She, however, could not control her curiosity and opened it. With that, all kinds of evils, such as diseases, also escaped into the world.

 Why was the Greek god Atlas punished by Zeus?

According to Greek mythology, Zeus punished Atlas for fighting against the gods who lived on Mount Olympus. Atlas was doomed forever to carry the burden of the world and the heavens on his shoulders.

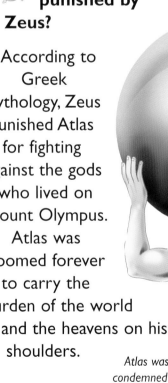

Atlas was condemned to carry the world on his shoulders

 Why did Athena, the Greek goddess of war, have no mother?

According to Greek legend, Athena sprang from her father Zeus's forehead as a full grown and fully armed warrior woman. Often depicted with a helmet and spear, she was also believed to be the goddess of wisdom.

 How was the Greek god Poseidon related to horses?

Poseidon, the Greek god of the sea, was also worshipped as Hippios, the god of horses. According to Greek legend, Poseidon was the father of the winged horse Pegasus, as well as the speaking horse, Arion.

Poseidon with his trident

The f hor. Pega

30

Which mythical Greek horse could fly?

According to Greek legend, the winged horse Pegasus flew up to Mount Olympus - the home of the gods. It was believed that Pegasus carried Zeus's thunderbolts.

How many eyes did the Cyclopes have?

The Cyclopes were Greek mythological giants who had only one eye in the middle of the forehead.

What weapon did the Greek god Zeus carry?

Zeus was a sky and weather god and also the supreme ruler of the deities of Mount Olympus. He carried the thunderbolt as his weapon.

Hermes, the winged messenger

Which legendary Greek god wore winged sandals and a winged cap?

Hermes, the messenger god, wore winged sandals and a winged cap. He also carried a magic wand crowned with wings.

FACT BOX

■ Artemis was the twin sister of Apollo, the Greek god of youth, beauty and light. Artemis was the goddess of the hunt, wild animals and childbirth. Both siblings were often depicted with a bow.

■ Argus was a mythical Greek monster with hundreds of eyes. After he was killed by the god Hermes, it is said that the goddess Hera decorated the tail of her peacock with Argus's eyes.

■ The ancient Greeks believed that their gods

A bowl of nectar

and goddesses ate ambrosia and drank nectar. It was thought that this food kept the gods young and strong.

MYTHOLOGY

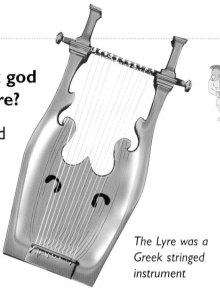

Which Greek god played the lyre?

Apollo, the god of truth, played a golden lyre. He was also called the god of healing and light.

The Lyre was a Greek stringed instrument

Which musical instrument did Athena invent?

Athena invented the flute but later threw it away. The Greeks believed that she invented the bridle too, so that man could tame horses.

Which Greek god rode a chariot drawn by dolphins?

Poseidon, the god of sea, rode a chariot drawn by dolphins. He carried a trident (three-pronged spear) that could shake the earth.

Where was the most famous oracle in ancient Greece?

Apollo's oracle at Delphi was the most famous one in ancien Greece. People believed that Apollo spoke to them through the priestess at the temple.

Whose kingdom was guarded by a three-headed, dragon-tailed creature?

Cerberus, a three-headed, dragon-tailed dog, guarded Hades' kingdom of the dead, the underworld.

The fierce monster Cerberus

LEGENDS AND HEROES

The ancient Greeks believed there were no gods in the beginning but only powerful beings called the Titans. The Titan king, Cronus, wanted to rule forever. However his son, Zeus, also wanted to be king. After defeating the Titans, he became the ruler of the universe.

The Greeks wove several stories and myths around their gods and goddesses.

Happy Family

Each of the gods wanted to be known as the most powerful. As a result they often fought among themselves. Sometimes they quarrelled with each other for the sake of humans too.

Gods on Earth

In some myths, the gods visited earth in different forms. Zeus turned himself into a bull in one legend and an eagle in another. The gods and goddesses could also curse humans and turn them into animals. Goddess Artemis is said to have turned a young man, Actaeon, into a deer.

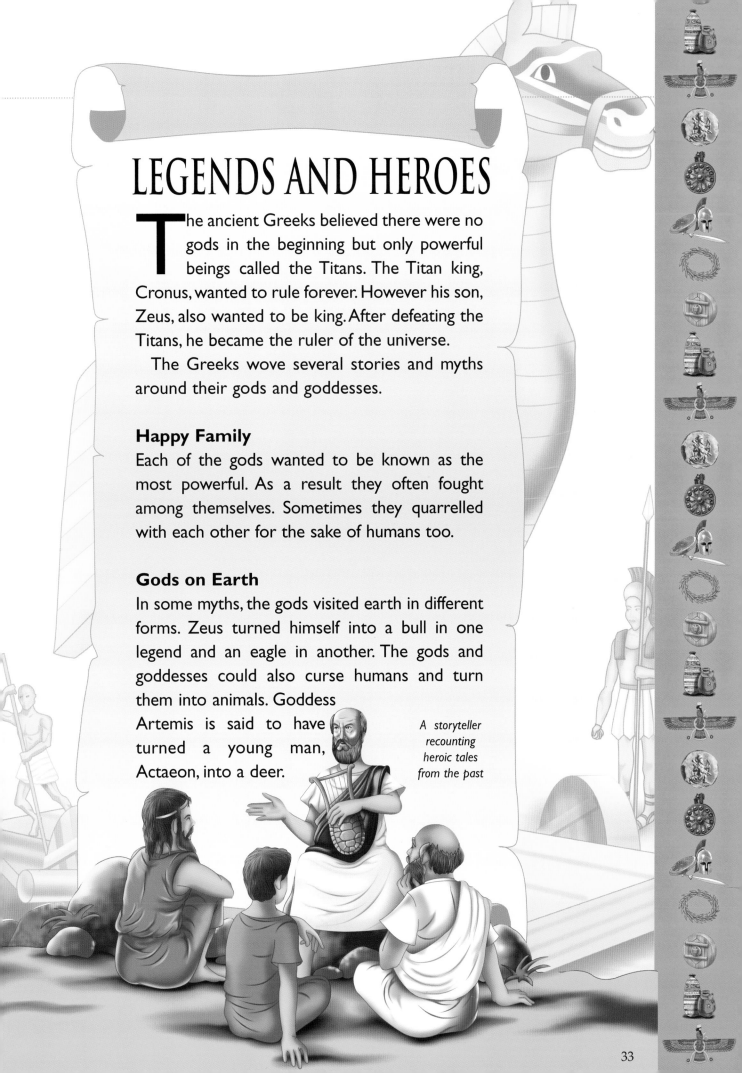

A storyteller recounting heroic tales from the past

LEGENDS AND HEROES

Were the centaurs human?

Centaurs were imaginary creatures with the head and upper body of a human and the lower body of a horse. They were usually unruly and violent but there was one just and wise centaur called Chiron.

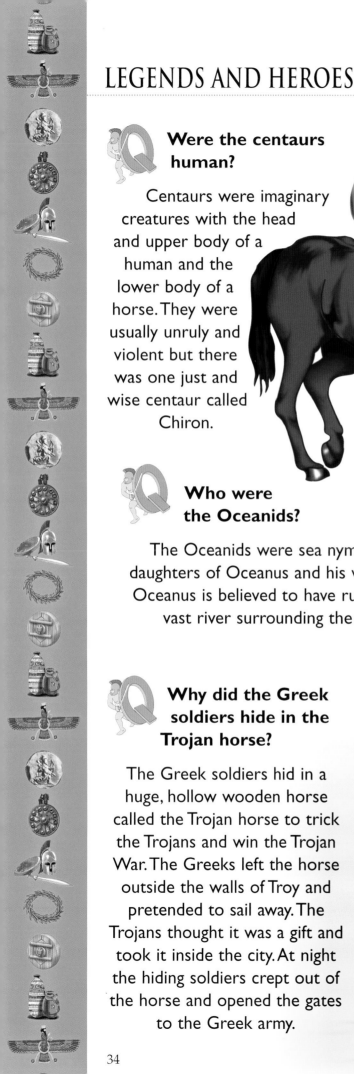

Centaurs were half man and half horse

Who were the Oceanids?

The Oceanids were sea nymphs and daughters of Oceanus and his wife Tethys. Oceanus is believed to have ruled over a vast river surrounding the earth.

Constructing the wooden Trojan horse

Why did the Greek soldiers hide in the Trojan horse?

The Greek soldiers hid in a huge, hollow wooden horse called the Trojan horse to trick the Trojans and win the Trojan War. The Greeks left the horse outside the walls of Troy and pretended to sail away. The Trojans thought it was a gift and took it inside the city. At night the hiding soldiers crept out of the horse and opened the gates to the Greek army.

How did Jason find the Golden Fleece?

In order to get back his kingdom Iolkos, the legendary Greek hero Jason had to find the Golden Fleece - the golden wool of a ram. He went on the ship Argo with a crew of men called the Argonauts. After many thrilling adventures, Jason found the Golden Fleece and brought it back to Iolkos.

The fearless Amazon queen

Who were the Amazons?

The Amazons were believed to be a tribe of fearless warrior women. According to a Greek myth one Amazon queen helped the Trojans during the Trojan War.

Why was Achilles's heel his weak spot?

According to Greek myth, Achilles was immersed in the River Styx by his mother to make him immortal. She held him by the heel while dipping him in the river. Therefor, the water did not touch Achilles's heel, making it his only weak spot. Later he died when his enemy Paris shot an arrow into his heel during the Trojan War.

FACT BOX

■ Greek myths say that Hephaestus, the Greek god of metalwork and fire, had his workshop beneath Mount Etna.

■ Hades, also known as Pluto, ruled the dead and was lord of the gloomy regions of the underworld. He was also believed to be the god of wealth because of the precious metals found in the depths of the earth.

■ The Phoenix was a Greek symbol of immortality and rebirth. This mythical bird was believed to reborn from its own ashes.

Rebirth of the Phoenix

LEGENDS AND HEROES

 Who had the head of a woman and the body of a bird?

The Sirens: Sailors who heard the songs of the Sirens used to lose control of their ships and usually died.

 How many heads and feet did Scylla, the sea monster, have?

Scylla had twelve feet and six heads, each with three rows of teeth. In Homer's epic, "The Odyssey", she is depicted as gobbling up six of Odysseus' sailors.

Whom did a white bull carry from Phoenicia to Crete?

Europa was carried to Crete on the back of Zeus, who had turned himself into a white bull.

Which young girl had snakes, instead of hair, on her head?

In Greek myth, a beautiful young girl called Medusa had snakes on her head. All her hair turned into snakes after she was cursed by Athena.

Medusa had live snakes on her head!

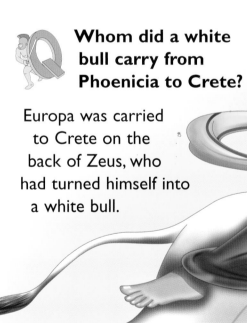

Europa on her way to Crete

ARMY

Wars were quite common in ancient Greece as the city-states often fought with each other. They were also attacked by foreigners.

A Greek battleship known as a trireme

Fighting Forces

While Sparta had the biggest army in Greece, Athens had the largest navy. The Athenians were famous for their fleet of warships called triremes. The Spartans were reputed to be fearless soldiers.

United We Win...

In 480 B.C. the Greek city-states joined together to fight the Persian forces led by King Xerxes. The powerful Greeks sent the Persians back after a crushing defeat.

Weapon-wise

Greek soldiers carried shields, spears and swords and wore bronze armour. They also wore special Corinthian helmets made from a single sheet of bronze. The armour and the helmets were padded with sea sponges.

Greek weapons

ARMY

What was siege warfare?

Siege warfare was a war scheme in which the Greek army would surround an enemy city and block the passage of goods and people. Eventually the city had to surrender because its supplies were cut off.

How did the Greek army enter an enemy fortress?

They used siege towers. These were large wooden platforms on wheels or rollers which could be placed high against the walls of the fortress. The invading Greek soldiers would then enter and capture the enemy.

Who was a hoplite?

A hoplite was a heavily armed foot soldier who belonged to the leading unit of the Greek army.

What weapons did a hoplite carry?

A hoplite's weapons were a long spear and a short double-bladed iron sword. His protective gear included a shield made of bronze and leather, a bronze helmet, a breastplate and leg guards.

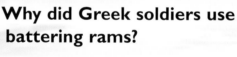

Why did Greek soldiers use battering rams?

A battering ram was a heavy wooden beam that was moved back and forth by Greek soldiers to rip through enemy gates and walls. It had a bronze, ram-shaped head from which it took its name. During sea battles the Greeks used the battering rams of their warships to destroy enemy vessels.

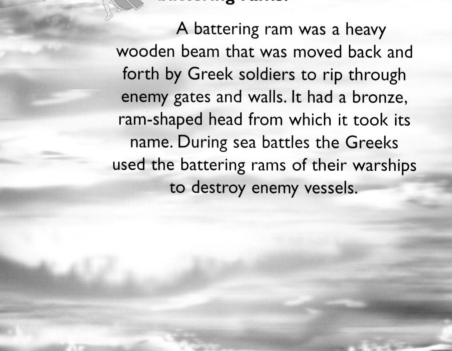

What was the shield carried by Greek hoplites called?

The shield was called the hoplon. It was a wooden bowl covered with bronze plates on the outside and leather on the inside. A hoplon could be as heavy as eight kilograms!

What was the armour worn by hoplites called?

The armour worn by hoplites was called the panoplia.

Greek soldiers ready to attack during a sea battle

FACT BOX

■ The trireme was an ancient Greek warship that had three rows of oars on each side. It had a battering ram on the bow with which it could smash into an enemy ship. These ships often displayed a painted eye that was believed to protect against bad luck.

■ In the fighting position, a Greek soldier stood with his spear raised above shoulder level.

■ The Greek army had supporting soldiers, called *psiloi*, who were armed with stones and clubs. The other supporting units consisted of archers and stone slingers.

A stone slinger

ARMY

Whose pictures did Athenian hoplites have on their hoplons?

Athenian hoplites usually had animal figures or pictures of gods painted on their hoplons. The Spartans, however, always had the Spartan symbol on their hoplon

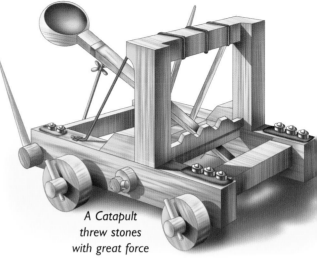

A Catapult
threw stones
with great force

Why did the Greek army form a phalanx?

A phalanx was made up of eight or more rows of hoplites. An injured or killed soldier was quickly replaced by the one behind him. A soldier carried his shield on his left arm. He was protected not only by his own shield, but also by the shield of the soldier on his right. As the soldiers moved shoulder to shoulder in a battlefield, they looked a fearsome sight indeed!

Why did the ancient Greeks use catapults in battles?

The Greek warships carried large catapults to fire stones at enemy ships.

How did the soldiers decorate their helmets?

The soldiers often decorated their helmets with crests of horsehair. The crests were made by fixing horsehair on to a block of wood.

How could an army defeat a phalanx?

An army could defeat a phalanx by either surrounding it from all sides or by breaking through its centre.

A military
formation called
the Phalanx

INVENTIONS AND DISCOVERIES

The Greeks were master craftsmen and skilled mathematicians. In fact, some of the earliest doctors and historians belonged to ancient Greece.

An early counting machine

Maths Mania

It is said that the Greeks calculated maths problems using pebbles and metal discs as counters. They moved these counters over marked boards to calculate answers. Did you know that the word "arithmetic" comes from the Greek "arithmos", which means number?

The Sun and the Stars

The Greeks noticed how some stars appeared to form patterns in the sky, and how the Moon changed its shape. They used their counters and boards to calculate how far the Moon is from Earth. The Greeks also suggested that the Earth was not flat, but round in shape.

The Greeks knew that the earth was a sphere

Medicine Men

Curing illnesses was considered to be a skill of the gods alone. The physician Asclepius was worshipped as a god by the ancient Greeks. Hippocrates, the famous physician, started practising in about 500 B.C.

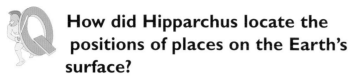

How did Hipparchus locate the positions of places on the Earth's surface?

The ancient Greek astronomer Hipparchus was the first person to locate the positions of places through a system of longitudes and latitudes. He suggested a zero longitude through the city-state of Rhodes.

Hipparchus calculating the longitude of Rhodes

Did the ancient Greeks know about the rotation and revolution of the Earth?

An ancient Greek, Aristarchus of Samos, is believed to be the first to propose that the Earth rotated on its own axis and revolved around the Sun.

What important theory about the moon did Anaxagoras propose?

The philosopher Anaxagoras made the first recorded claim that the light of the Moon was actually a reflection from the Sun. He was even arrested for declaring that the Sun was not a god but a massive burning stone.

What theory did the Greek scientist Ptolemy propose?

The Greek scientist Ptolemy wrote in the *Almagest* that the Earth was the centre of the universe and also that the stars and other planets moved around it. This theory was later disproved.

Which physician god's symbol was a serpent wrapped around a staff?

The symbol of a serpent wrapped around a staff was attributed to Asclepius, the Greek god of healing. It is believed that in ancient Greece snakes were often used to make ointments!

Serpent wrapped round a staff

Who is the Hippocratic Oath associated with?

The Hippocratic Oath was named after the physician Hippocrates, regarded as the "Father of Medicine". Graduating medical students often take the Hippocratic Oath of observing the duties and principles of their profession.

A Greek physician

Which famous ancient Greek collected and studied plants?

The famous philosopher Aristotle collected samples of plants and studied them. This marked the beginning of the science of botany.

FACT BOX

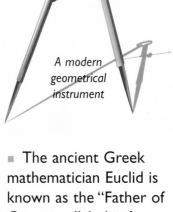

A modern geometrical instrument

■ The ancient Greek mathematician Euclid is known as the "Father of Geometry". In his famous book 'Elements,' he proved hundreds of geometry principles.

■ The Greek scientist Eratosthenes is regarded as the first person to measure the distance around the Earth.

■ It is believed that the ancient Greeks knew how to melt iron in furnaces. Apparently, they also made steel by adding carbon to iron.

INVENTIONS AND DISCOVERIES

Why did Archimedes run down the street shouting "Eureka"?

Archimedes was an important Greek mathematician. One day, while having a bath, he found a solution to a problem that had been bothering him. He was so excited that he ran out into the streets naked, shouting "Eureka" ("I have found it").

Which Greek philosopher was punished for not respecting the gods?

Socrates was punished by law on the charge of disrespecting the gods. Many people of that age felt uncomfortable with his ideas of logic and reason.

How did the ancient Greeks keep time?

The ancient Greeks used water clocks. During public speeches they often timed the speakers using these clocks.

Archimedes, the ancient Greek genuis

Measuring time with water

Why did the ancient Greeks visit a place called the Asclepion?

People visited the Asclepion to pray for good health. The Asclepion was a temple dedicated to Asclepius. Such temples were built at several places, including Athens and Corinth.